"One of the most promising young poet-critics in America."
–*Los Angeles Times*

"Philosophically engaged rather than philosophically detached, Adam Kirsch brings a singular and welcome seriousness to contemporary verse. In his new collection, he trains a shrewd eye on the violence and vulgarity of our age, but also celebrates, intelligently and convincingly, the larger and enduring realities of art, science, peace, and faith. These excellent poems are triumphs of craft and hope."
–TIMOTHY STEELE

"In these unusually thoughtful, elegant poems, Adam Kirsch has consistently achieved the same end as the 'hypothetical' light of the collection's sole sonnet: he has 'made our dark matter visible.'"
–JACQUELINE OSHEROW

"One of the things that is so impressive and exciting about Kirsch's work is his use of a contemporary idiom that is also traditional.... This is a recipe for a poetic language capable of handling elevated themes in our present culture. Dante called it the *volgare illustre*, heightened vernacular, and it is good news that Adam Kirsch is trying to realize...such writing in contemporary America."
–ANDREW FRISARDI, *Los Angeles Times*

D1043036

Invasions

Invasions

POEMS

Adam Kirsch

Ivan R. Dee, Chicago

www.ivanrdee.com

Library of Congress Cataloging-in-Publication Data:
Kirsch, Adam, 1976–
  Invasions : poems / Adam Kirsch.
    p. cm.
  ISBN-13: 978-1-56663-774-9 (alk. paper)
  ISBN-10: 1-56663-774-0 (alk. paper)
  I. Title.
  PS3611.I77I58 2008
  811'.6–dc22   2007039421

To Remy

CONTENTS

PART ONE

When only birds keep up the traffic where   5
Outlet Mall in Western Massachusetts   6
The tin balls that the Planetarium   7
The Gothic silhouette and flying spire   8
The Cloisters Chapel   9
The one thing needful to the Gallery   10
The prayers the Congregationalists read   11
Sing-Along "Messiah," Disney Hall   12
Whether the carapace of reverence   13
Wolfman, Ratman   14
A narrow strip of darker cinnamon   15
The usual soundtrack for the gallery   16
How many West Side classic sixes were   17
The flat scratch of the mono microphone   18
Opera Night at Caffe Taci   19
Soixante-neuf, année érotique   20
Larkin   21
Wordsworth   22
Even a mother's undissuadable   23
To Marnie   24
The Masonic Temple   25
No journey whose first step is in a file   26
Now that no one looking at the night   27
After the rabbi's game repeating back   28
Hip-hop's favorite furrier, who dyes   29
Having no bodies, they will understand   30

PART TWO

The Consolations   33

PART THREE

September fifteenth, and the house is full 43
The long, squat, leaden-windowed, burrow-like 44
Calmly, the papers calculate the chance 45
Withdrawal 46
Only the pace of innovation spared 47
April 2003 48
Knowing that some Army engineer 49
The stripes of smoke describing an oblique 50
Two Views of Napoleon by David 51
Once the first infant's taken by the heel 52
Between the baronial townhouse, holding fast 53
Past the off-duty NYPD guard 54
Jewish Community Center, Amsterdam and 74th 55
The shame-demented villager who stands 56
The injured silence of the immigrant 57
The malefactors of the '90s make 58
Palgrave's Golden Treasury 59
The disappearance of the lines of force 60
The windows painted shut and gradually 61

Acknowledgments 63

Invasions

I.

When only birds keep up the traffic where
The grounded helicopters used to dive
With fly-eyes and decapitating hair
In stories they have heard and half-believe,
And men are forced to dig out silted wells
To take the place of ancient pipes that broke
And cannot be repaired, and women fill
The double buckets biting on their necks,
What will they find more comforting? Contempt
For bankrupt fathers, superstitious fear
Of visitors who built these ziggurats
Then took to rumored ships and disappeared,
Or pride in their untraceable descent
From men who knew that hospitality
At the gods' tables is impermanent
And pitiless, as gods are meant to be?

OUTLET MALL IN WESTERN MASSACHUSETTS

The broad sky seeping shadow, and the hills
Retreating under blackened canopies
Looked just as alien when evening fell,
In Jonathan Edwards' lamplit century,
On Indian Stockbridge, in its palisade
Of shaved logs sharpened into anxious spears.
The only difference is the clearing, paved
In asphalt parking lots and ranks of stores,
Huddled all night in a fluorescent nest
More proof against the dark than any fort.
Whether the bargain-hunters and the tourists
Want half of what they're heaping in their carts,
Nobody knows or asks; tonight as ever
We do compulsively what must be done
To make ourselves forget the drowning river,
The hoarse owl, and the forest closing in.

The tin balls that the Planetarium
Displays to demonstrate the powers of ten
Range from the pebbly fraction of an atom
To a hot air balloon that means the sun,
Indicting cosmologically provincial
Habits they can't help but reinforce
By tailoring their exponential spiral
To the perspective of an audience
Whose unraised power is thereby made to seem
The integer of all created things.
Where is the diorama that could shame
And reconcile a creature that belongs
In the dark bowel of the universe
Only as our insides accommodate
Weird flora whose unconscious processes
We never see and couldn't live without?

The Gothic silhouette and flying spire
Address the campus with a confidence
Inherited from buttresses and choirs
Adapted to the Catholic skies of France.
If at the swinging summons of the bell
The snow-blind distance gradually revealed
A feudal Sunday's lost processional
Of ox-drawn peasants and their mounted lord,
It would be less surprising than the sight
Of so few Christians in these ranks of pews,
Who gather out of homesickness or habit
To hear the echoes of the old good news—
Waiting until the concrete dorms decay
For these stone arches' rediscoverer
To envy or regret the certainty
Of dead parishioners that never were.

THE CLOISTERS CHAPEL

Whether the censer-swinging celebrant
Would process calmly up the center aisle
That Rockefeller paid to replicate
Down to the altar-screen in Norman style,
Or stumble, noticing behind the blue
Infusion of the Virgin's plate-glass gown
The piled-up tourist steamers muscling through
The Hudson to the concrete piers of Midtown,
The count whose pillage and extortion paid
The masons who set stone on perfect stone
And artisans who piously inlaid
Thick stripes of color in the windowpane
Would soon be reassured to recognize
That Standard Oil's equation was his own:
The deeper that the iron drill-bit bites,
The higher shoots the rare, expensive plume.

The one thing needful to the Gallery
Of Bible Art that stands unvisited
And unabashed among the lights of Broadway
Wasn't the funds the church solicited
From corporate endowments or its rich
Midwestern sectaries, but ignorance
Of the impression that its pious kitsch
Would make on those who aren't congregants,
Like the twelve demonstrators who unroll
A banner, "NewYorkAtheists.com,"
And tape their Xeroxed fliers to the marble
Frieze of Bible heroes with a grim,
Impassioned disrespect inherited
From the first Christian pickets to protest
The temples of the gods they knew were dead,
No matter how much the embalming cost.

The prayers the Congregationalists read
Beside the grave-hole of Elizabeth
Who lasted sixteen months and John who died
At eighty-one the patriarchal death
His offspring and his acreage had earned
Were equally impersonal, as plain
As the small steeple whose white stroke affirmed
That each reward or punishment had been
Decided somewhere else, and long before.
Whether the widow could believe that heaven,
Or if the shaking mother had preferred
Not to give back so soon what she'd been given,
The mottoes on the tablets do not say;
Nor does it matter, now that faith and doubt
Are swallowed up in the same victory,
This summer churchyard full of finished plots.

SING-ALONG "MESSIAH," DISNEY HALL

The rosewood organ pipes, two stories tall,
Are skewed according to the architect's
Taste for the mischievous diagonal;
Better this giant's game of pick-up-sticks,
He seems to tell us, than the sturdily
Hierarchical ensemble in the church
Where the composer made these burgherly
Chorales in celebration of the birth
Of a Redeemer perched upon a throne
At the same altitude from which the choir
Would pour down on the silent congregation
Expert harmonies. These volunteers
Who launch themselves into the "Comfort ye,"
Following in the scores they brought from home,
Produce the less angelic harmony
Of singers comforting themselves alone.

Whether the carapace of reverence
The nuclear family wore protectively
Was justified for sheltering arrangements
We needed in an age of scarcity
When weakling sons would happily prostrate
Themselves before the father-tyrant whose
Impostures they could not afford to hate
As long as he knocked down their enemies
With the same fist he flourished in their faces,
It now looks no more permanent than ponds
Debris creates by damming up the courses
Of rivers whose one impulse is to spend
Themselves in spurts of foam and dissipate,
Now that we've learned to disobstruct ourselves
Of everything unsuited to our fate
As brains in jars that have no relatives.

WOLFMAN, RATMAN

Once there could have been no milder sight
Than this, so early it was always known—
The child would fall asleep to candlelight
And father straining at his mother's groan,
Notes in the nightsong like the ruffling thatch
And beckoning of crickets. Safety rose
Like vapor from their flesh that was his flesh,
The rhythm swayed him, and his eyes would close.
There has been some great estrangement. What else brings
These baffled victims to the doctor's couch
To learn the true identities of things
Transformed by nightmare into tooth and pouch,
And understand they hurt themselves to spite
The parents whose old wantonness destroyed
Their childish confidence against the rat
Obscenely dragging, and the wolf's slit eye?

A narrow strip of darker cinnamon
Traces a border on the parquet floor:
One of the insignificant, uncommon
Details from that vague era called prewar
In *Douglas Elliman's* sleek, provoking slang,
For which the postwar-prosperous compete;
The sort of luxury that draws a pang
From the ultramodern complex down the street.
Not until later do they notice how
The border runs wrong-angled in the hall
And vanishes, the careful pattern now
Sectioned to incoherence by the wall
That carved the unit from the one next door.
The expectation of unbroken lines
And unearned spaciousness is gone; no more
The ordinary life of large design.

The usual soundtrack for the gallery
Of Dutch Old Masters is made up of mild
Dramatic "Ohs" of sensibility,
The droning commentary of self-styled
Experts on the period, the buzz
Escaping muffled from the headphone tour.
It is another, more insistent noise
That fills the room with agitated whispers:
He's here, we learn without quite being told,
The almost-of-the-first-rank movie star,
Who, though his famous roles are ten years old,
Can still outdraw a Rembrandt or Vermeer;
No face glazed brown or bathed in lemony,
Perfected light can hold us as we steal
Next door, compelled by what we came to see—
The bearer of the magically real.

How many West Side classic sixes were
Exchanged for Delray Beach amenities
Or curtained cellblocks in extended care
Or the cemetery-tenements of Queens
To yield the plunder of their double-shelved,
Floor-to-ceiling libraries to stock
The shabby Park Slope bookshops that preserve
Their silver age in broken paperbacks
Of Forster's *Two Cheers for Democracy*,
And Freud on dreams, and Philip Rieff on Freud,
And Trilling's "exigent" apology
For the dilemmas of the liberal mind—
The scriptures of a time more serious,
Whose sectaries won't congregate again,
Outside these aisles, to praise and criticize
The majestic ambivalence of Henry James.

The flat scratch of the mono microphone
And ambient hissing as the tape unspools
Are not more antiquated than the song,
Whose tame exuberance is early Beatles,
Just post-Ed Sullivan, pre-Abbey Road.
Already there is something Greensleeves-like
In the lilting of "I Wanna Hold Your Hand";
What tells the future is the roaring static
Barely discernible as wild applause:
Pure self-assertion of an audience
Exalted past the object of their praise,
A volume-click away from violence.
After that riot of united will,
How could the '60s audience retrieve
The harmony of individuals
Clapping in ragged time on "Bye Bye Love"?

OPERA NIGHT AT CAFFE TACI

No curtains here, no chandelier to raise;
She takes the low stage and begins to peal
Long airs of anguish, to distracted praise
From the gourmands of opera and the meal.
She wears the helium shoulderpads of dresses
Sold in a suburban bridal shop,
Rigid in velvet, while the waitresses
Lounge at their ease in cottons from the Gap;
Whatever third-rate coach she studied with
Could not undo the mannerism that
Half-shuts her eyes and splays her lipsticked mouth,
The cartoon mincing of a marionette.
It's all just as it should be. For the crowd,
The sensual pampering and dignified
Consumption; in return she is allowed
To sing, gauche and ignored, beatified.

SOIXANTE-NEUF, ANNÉE ÉROTIQUE

When rationed gaslight, pillaged vintages,
And the best tables at the cabaret
Were kept for those conscripted villagers
Promoted by their occupiers' gray
From beer and waltzes to the *vie bohème*,
No wonder Paris hummed itself the tunes
Chevalier put over with the same
Old coziness and antebellum croon
That said *Paris sera toujour Paris.*
They suffered so their sons could realize
The profits of the liberation, free
To coax Jane Birkin's paradisal sighs
From daughters with long hair and *mini-jupes*
Whose mothers covered up their shaven heads—
From '44, the year of rising up,
To '69, the year of getting laid.

LARKIN

What the average sensual man cannot forgive
Or triumph over, slowly he forgets;
By thirty-five or so begins to live
With the faint metal taste of choked regret
Flavoring every swallow. For romance
He'll never find with girls he'll never meet,
And plutocratic ease in the south of France,
And the shouted homage of a trembling street,
He learns in time to substitute a wife,
Two weeks' vacation, the "respect of peers":
The prolonged catastrophe we call a life
Instead of the coming true of our worst fears.
If genius is to carry the pristine
Shock of perception to the bitter last,
There was no purer genius: philistine,
Uncompromising, foul mouth stuffed with rust.

WORDSWORTH

The cases sweating in the flower shop
Preserve the daisy, lesser celandine,
And other stragglers banished from the strip
That blooms along the Broadway median,
Whose fume-assaulted corridor is kept
Less as a landscape to get lost inside
Than as a scrap of litmus paper, dipped
Into the changing weather to provide
Chemical confirmation of the spring;
Or a St. Patrick's ribbon that declares
Allegiance to a country never seen;
Or homeopathic remedy that cures
With just a droplet where a dose would kill.
Your deep lung would have suffocated where
This April morning seems to give us all
We need or want, whose breaths are shallower.

Even a mother's undissuadable,
Unlimited expectation couldn't see
In Austin, ten years old and six feet tall,
More than a magnet for the cruelty
Of all the averagely developed boys
Whose gravitation tugged him to a slouch,
Or hear in Paula's homeroom rhapsodies
About her depth and specialness, the rich
Unguessed-at inner life she had to share,
More than an awkward phase that she'd outgrow.
Seeing her now, spead-eagled on a cover
To advertise her new one-woman show,
Or him sink baskets on ESPN,
They seem to wear the self-suspecting smile
Of understudies ordered to fill in
For grown-ups who stepped out a little while.

TO MARNIE

Maybe you think the bargain tacitly
Promoted at the pet adoption booth
Of food for love offends your dignity,
Or maybe you were never taught that teeth
Aren't the right way to express affection;
You won't sit still, unless you're half asleep,
For even the most guarded grooming session,
But use your hind legs and your jaw to clamp
Our scratched-up, well-intentioned hands as far
As possible from your defended belly,
Whose fur conceals the pucker of a scar
Someone or something gave you in the alley
You think you're going back to every time
You hear a car pass or the front door open,
And hook your swaying tail into an emblem
Of an old fear's unanswerable question.

THE MASONIC TEMPLE

When the blindfold is removed, and candlelight
Picks out the faces in the smoky lodge,
The giddiness of the initiate
Sours to disbelief, and then outrage–
The master of the thirty-third degree
Sold him his car insurance, and the car
Was haggled from the sharp adept that he
Kneeled down with reverently before the altar.
Worst of all is the obvious relief
With which they put away the trowel and square
To settle at the level of themselves–
And that he's happier in that atmosphere
Of eating, drinking, dealing, telling jokes.
He falls so quickly that he couldn't say
Whether he feels himself more of a fake
With or without the apron's dignity.

No journey whose first step is in a file
So meek and orderly that, shuffling
Along the jetway as into a jail,
They seem to think that God is bargaining
A safe arrival for their good behavior,
Could end somewhere worth going. In the taste
Of ozone-stale, recirculated air,
In taxiing that gathers to a blast
For which a hundred takeoffs don't prepare,
Is something worse than fear: the helplessness
Of carried things that cannot move themselves.
Such literal pursuit of foreignness
Brings what the airplane traveler deserves;
But not for them the new, familiar face,
The streets that coil to mazes in the rain,
The choirs and arches gathering a peace,
Of people, towns, cathedrals never seen.

Now that no one looking at the night-
Sky blanked by leakage from electric lamps
And headlights prowling through the parking lot
Could recognize the Babylonian dance
That once held every gazer; now that spoons
And scales, and swordsmen battling with beasts
Have decomposed into a few stars strewn
Illegibly across an empty space,
Maybe the old unfalsifiable
Predictions and extrapolated spheres
No longer need to be an obstacle
To hearing what it is the stars declare:
That there are things created of a size
We can't and weren't meant to understand,
As fish know nothing of the sun that writes
Its bright glyphs on the black waves overhead.

After the rabbi's game repeating back
Of anecdotes he heard an hour before,
But edited to bland endorsements like
Those on a dating-service questionnaire—
Funny, liked to travel, good with kids—
How can he ask the mourners to believe
In anything he says the Psalmist said?
The euphemism of eternal life,
Received in awkward silence like the false
Prognosis used to keep the patient calm,
We let go by politely; what consoles
Is this true image of the World to Come:
The jostle of the pine box on the straps
Slackening as the diggers turn a crank,
The mourners shoveling the streaky clumps
That scatter with a soft unanswered knock.

Hip-hop's favorite furrier, who dyes
A poncho braided from a hundred minks
The copyrighted blue of Tiffany's,
Is one of the idealists who think
Civilization's a trajectory
Away from nature, like the silhouette
Of whalebone-powered antigravity
Cast by the wigs of Marie Antoinette
That broke impertinently from the plane
Where hair extrudes instinctively from skulls
And farmers tediously sow the grain
The chef makes levitate in his soufflés;
His is the helplessness of artists who,
Deformed by the division of their labor,
Will be the most missed but the first to go
When civilization ends and we start over.

Having no bodies, they will understand
Things like the keyboard or the steering wheel—
All instruments adapted to the hand,
Which by that time will be vestigial
For them, as gills and flippers are for us—
Only as bad translators of desire
From what was once the mind to what was once
The world outside it. Nor will they admire
The error messages that we produce
Each time the incompatibility
Between the two is registered as loss,
Even if our frustrated vanity
Names those malfunctions art. Imagining
The perfect signals they will have become,
It's more and more impossible to think
That anything we write's addressed to them.

II.

THE CONSOLATIONS

after Boethius

II.7 *Quicumque solam mente praecipiti petit*

Obsolete as the ornamental sword
And stylized codpiece of the courtier,
The masculine ambition to secure
Something like deathlessness by deeds or words.

The crown of laurel and the diadem,
Now shorn of plausibility, are like
The hypertrophic antlers of the elk,
Crippling the bull-head that demanded them:

What else were Caesar and Napoleon
But Dahmers on a continental scale?
The more vainglorious the general,
The better if he never had been born.

Stupider, and therefore less to blame,
Are the civilians of celebrity,
Ephemerids of movies and TV,
Millionaire heroes of steroidal games;

For these, the height of glamour is to earn
The right to have their sex lives analyzed
In English, Urdu, Greek and Japanese,
Until next year it's someone younger's turn.

No matter how promiscuous, their fame
Will not console them in their dying hour;
All they have done is multiply death's power:
When they're forgotten, they will die again.

III.2 *Quantas rerum flectat habenas*

Bend back the sapling till it stubs
    Leaves in the dirt;
Soon as you let it go, it snaps
    Fiercely upright.

Make the tame lion beg his food
    From human hands;
Once he has smelled the trainer's blood,
    There's no defense.

And if the moon in private dreams
    That she's a planet,
Still every sunset she resumes
    Her slavish orbit.

Inertia, instinct, gravity—
    By any name
The power condemning them to be
    Always the same

Governs us with a law as strong,
    Which we call evil,
Saying we won't escape for long
    Our own dead level.

III.7 *Habet hoc voluptas omnis*

First the hypnosis
As the hive buzzes,
Issuing dank and honeyed promises;

Lust for the rose-
Gold-tinted ooze
Makes you forget the swarm, the sting, the bruise.

IV.4 *Quid tantos iuvat excitare motus*

They must believe a stroke's too mild,
    A heart attack too slow,
AIDS too easy to avoid,
    Tumors hard to grow;

The way these soldiers swap their youth
    For uniforms and guns,
They must think God has given death
    A less than sporting chance.

IV.3 *Vela Neritii ducis*

Circe who gloated to observe
The sailors grunting for their slop,
Their tournaments of tusk and hoof,
Their cocks' bewildered corkscrew droop,

Had less imagination than
Whatever sorcerer concealed
Under so many shapes of men
Souls that were made to rut and squeal.

II:4 *Quisquis volet perennem*

The man who cannot hope to own
A house unless he takes a loan
He'll still be paying off when he
Is on Social Security
Might daydream of a terraced perch
On Venice or Miami Beach,
Watching the wave that scours and breaks
In sizzling phosphorescent flakes,
Swimming naked in a balmy
California January,
Breathing Floridian perfume
Of sunscreen, alcohol and brine;
But then, remembering the jolt
Preparing in the coastal fault,
The timber-smashing wind and rain
Of yearly Force Five hurricanes,
He thinks it wiser to invest
In the dry, steady, flat Midwest,
Where a small plot of solid ground
Won't lift you up or let you down.
So when the great catastrophe
Arrives, he'll watch it on TV,
See pixilated fire or flood
Destroy his almost-neighborhood,
And piously reiterate
His law of life and real estate:
The best investment's one that earns
Small but reliable returns.

I.5 *O stelliferi conditor orbis*

The jag and hover of the bee
Comes on him uncontrollably;
In his complete obedience
Is nothing that intends the dance.

The seed that goes to bed in spring
Wakes up in time for harvesting,
Although the summer didn't choose
To shrink the night and warm the breeze.

The universe itself can't know
Its calibrated ratios,
Though it would crumple in or fall
Apart at a misplaced decimal.

If such unvarying success
Is guaranteed to mindlessness,
What could explain or justify
The negligence that made us free?

V.3 *Quaenam discors foedera rerum*

Something is missing. When the telescope
Anxiously scans a sector of the night,
The numbers streaming in do not add up;
The universe would be too cold or hot,
Too dense or empty, if it weren't for
Dimensions that won't let themselves be caught.
Why is it that this absence reassures?
Dividing what we know by what we see,
We always find that permanent remainder,
The margin of an old perplexity
Now justified and even rational;
For somewhere, it is certain, there must be
The light, remembered, hypothetical,
That once made our dark matter visible.

III.

September fifteenth, and the house is full;
It seems few patrons died or stayed at home.
The City Opera, brave, professional,
Reminds us and themselves the show goes on.
Ash drifting north has left a coat so thin
The cladded travertine still glitters white,
And so mild no one coughs to breathe it in
On the hot breeze of a late summer night—
What I call ash, but know to be this face,
Snapshotted, Xeroxed, stapled to a pole,
Which every breath I take helps to erase
And scatter incorporate in a new whole.
But what air isn't filled with old remains
Like these, and infinitely multiplied?
What did they die for but our ignorance
Of the ways and times and reasons that they died?

The long, squat, leaden-windowed, burrow-like
Offices terracing the Palisades
Seem the earliest architecture, such as make
On Afghan mountains bombproof barricades—
Or anywhere a Third World tenantry
Survives our televised annihilation
By clamping down and taking root. To see
On the Hudson echoes of that habitation
Once could provoke humility, the theme
For abstract reveries that all is flux.
Staring across the river now, it seems
A sign of how civilization self-destructs:
Their single-minded virtuous contempt,
Our bashful Alexandrian tolerance,
Our glass towers and their common, huddling, cramped,
Impregnable cliffside. We don't stand a chance.

Calmly, the papers calculate the chance
That in ten years the planet and a shard
Of rock will consummate the long romance
We've led with ruin. This will be ignored:
Not for the small but lotto-beating odds,
But from the madman's counterfactual ease
That fissions us as always into gods
Who count in aeons and eternities,
And beasts who scavenge for the daily kill,
Gobbling down the meat that will not keep.
Does the beast suspect that nuclear winter will
Be secretly welcome as untroubled sleep,
And does the god observe the sky in peace
Since his life neither starts nor ends in weather?
Both let what will come come; for the decrees
Of the asteroid are righteous altogether.

WITHDRAWAL

The good it did was negative. The mail
Put off its weaponized white coat of spores;
The jets no longer seemed about to fall
Or pivot madly toward the upper floors;
Such things returned to their old habitat
In nightmares and the crawl on CNN.
But where did the rainbow come from, pledging that
The flood subsiding wouldn't rise again?
It was just something swallowed with the dose
That fed the brain its missing chemicals,
Coaxing it from its darker purposes
Back to the daylight we assume is normal.
Now as the milligrams decrease, the ache
And sizzle of the synapse slowing down
Warns that these months of peace were a mistake;
Things were not wrong inside, but all around.

Only the pace of innovation spared
The Paris of Haussmann, Wilhelmine Berlin
The megatons they would have been prepared
To deal and be dealt, rather than give in
On a single point of acreage or pride.
Europe it was that taught the world to kill
Immensely and believe it justified.
What Alsace couldn't bring, the Kashmir will;
By summer's end, we'll see the border crossed
By massed divisions mustered on the brink.
The hopeful think ten million will be lost,
And Europe urges reason, gorged on luck.
We wake these days into the total calm
Known to the fugitive as he gives up,
The ratchet of the roller coaster's climb
Into the sudden, nauseating drop.

APRIL 2003

Because tomorrow they will be replaced
By dead celebrities of another war,
Remember them now, ennobled or disgraced
By endings greater than they bargained for.
The girl who in another time had played
Cow-eyed Briseis, meek and victimized,
Emptied her clip till captured, and was freed
By comradeship in chivalry's disguise.
Their tyrant's bodyguard who lost his tongue
For hinting where our missiles should be sent;
Our ensign that a nameless grievance stung
To heave a bomb into his captain's tent;
Last, the embedded editor who rolled
His Humvee to the bottom of a dune,
And lost the story. Now that they are told,
Forget them, since there will be others soon.

Knowing that some Army engineer
Was charged with calculating how to stack
For maximum efficiency the soldiers'
Corpses in the plane that brings them back;
That someone requisitioned all these flags
Tied diaper-like around each cedar box,
And drew up estimates for body bags
And must revise them after each attack;
That someone seated on a forklift caught
Each coffin roughly in its iron prongs,
And dropped it on the pile; and that a guard
Is sealed up with the dead the whole flight long;
Knowing that all of these and hundreds more
Collaborate to help each soldier die,
Who could declare the necessary war?
Ignorance is responsibility.

The stripes of smoke describing an oblique,
Too steeply angled flight path seem to veer
Like homing pigeons toward the North Atlantic,
Till the wind rises and they start to blur.
They leave no trace but a distinct impression
Of more than civilian altitude and speed—
Not the LaGuardia-bound Airbuses flashing
Crosses of landing lights just overhead,
But something that technology's stripped down
To a stub-winged and pilotless syringe
That doesn't hesitate or ask permission
To consummate its supersonic plunge,
Lingering only in its passage higher
To draw these advertisements in the sky
For a new kind of combat that requires
Us only not to notice or ask why.

TWO VIEWS OF NAPOLEON BY DAVID

The horse, distracted by a pebble-spill
That rattles down the cliff-face and explodes
In volleys like a rain of musketballs,
Rears up in panic as his eye protrudes
With noticing so many ways to die.
Knowing that what defines the hero is
The magnitude of what he doesn't see,
The rider flings his arm and turns his face
Toward the unpeopled, unobstructed blue;
Blue that returns, but darker now, in drapes
That dim the study where he pages through
His drafts and memos, crossing out mistakes,
His sword-arm tucked inside a straining vest
And face gone slack with resignation, having
Realized too late that what he's forced
To care about, or try to, makes the king.

Once the first infant's taken by the heel
And swung by laughing soldiers so his brain
Cracks like an egg against the ghetto wall,
The name of the Father isn't named again;
Then we demand the Judge, who may not save
But metes out the reward and punishment.
We stop petitioning when we observe
The peaceful old age of the commandant,
Teaching us that we must be satisfied
With a Recorder who lets nothing slip—
Till human bones that human teeth have chewed
Or throat-slit mummies in a frozen Alp
Resurface to remind us of the million
Victims that decompose for each preserved,
And that the mute Accuser is the one
God we might still believe in or deserve.

Between the baronial townhouse, holding fast
To obsolete aloofness though obscured
By sky-dividing neighbors, and the vast
Development less built than engineered,
These brownstones hold the balance. In the late
Midsummer sunlight, deepening to blue,
They file away, bourgeois, companionate,
At shoulder height down West End Avenue.
They were made for this: a living-room recital
Where a semi-professional, semi-retired,
Entirely serious pianist, despite all
Infirmities of age, can be admired
By her serious lawyer, teacher, doctor friends.
The Jewish reverence for each German note
Remember, when this latest refuge ends
And all the lamps are shattered or put out.

Past the off-duty NYPD guard,
Next to the cardboard box of old *kippoth*,
A Plexiglas display case holds a scarred
Deconsecrated scroll, above a note:
Seized by the Nazis, 1941.
Of course the word is here: what synagogue
But stands in memory of what they've done?
Intact in Little Neck or burnt in Prague,
We braid the four hooked letters of their name
With our outnumbered three. How is it more
Or all of us are not bent back and lame
Like the old beadle swaying by the door?
Maybe what saves us is the nervous hum
That rises, like a second, truer prayer,
From the gossiping, distracted congregation,
Murmuring to itself: still here, still here.

JEWISH COMMUNITY CENTER, AMSTERDAM AND 74TH

What happened in the shadow of the wall
Daubed with a mural of the *Judensau*
Took on the cramped, conspiratorial,
Imaginary aspect of the Jew
Conjectured by the citizens who passed
The ghetto tollgate, no more curious
To see inside than their descendants, faced
With the prefabricated, windowless
Showers with furnaces that smoked all day.
The cure is meant to be transparent walls
Through which they watch us talk, drink coffee, pray,
Safe in the light like everybody else;
Except this proof of ostentatious trust
Is underwritten by the barricades
Planted at curbside to deflect the blast
From which we have forgotten how to hide.

The shame-demented villager who stands
His shared-out, used-up daughter to the wall
In some veiled province of Afghanistan
And shrieks the rocks on till her body falls
Has more in common with the baritone
Who sends Lucia intricately mad
Than the applauding Metropolitan
Opera season-ticket-holding crowd,
Whose sympathy for teenage girls seduced
Like Gilda by a horny head of state
Is equal to their openmindedness
Toward Violetta-like ex-prostitutes,
Neither of whom would have to be afraid
Of impoliteness at their dinner table;
Only the shedding of a woman's blood
Made holiness and honor possible.

The injured silence of the immigrant
Who tunneled under homicidal braids
Of wire that a flirtatious government
Adorns the border with like necklace beads
Is not so much the amputation scar
Of skies cut off and cousins left behind,
As the stigmata of the bitterer
Discovery his country doesn't mind
Or notice one name missing from the census.
To see the parting blessing camouflaged
In that cold tolerance of absence is
Reserved for those denied the privilege
Of feeling their departure's not desertion,
Who read in certain catastrophic headlines
The silent notice of their reconscription
To wars they only thought they left behind.

The malefactors of the '90s make
Their last appearance on the TV news
With a docility that would have struck
Their mustard-gassed and gunned-down victims as
An answer to the prayers they couldn't stop
Themselves addressing to discredited
Promoters of a peace they couldn't keep,
The heavenly and the blue-helmeted.
The thing that would be harder to explain
To them than the delayed, improbable
Reprisal that found out Saddam Hussein
And killed Milosevic inside his cell
Is the unanimous indifference
That greets the latest spectacle of nations
Driven by their offended impotence
To murder those by whom offenses come.

While gangster nobles sowed the glebe with pain
That peasants were condemned to reap, because
Their pride committed them to those inane
Badges, the bloody and the bled-dry rose;
While bishops in the Tower were martyrized
For creeds their congregations couldn't spell,
And pure Dissenters saw the unbaptized
In an eagerly delineated Hell;
While country families sent their duller sons
To keep an empire's neck under the boot,
And city millionaires extracted fortunes
From showers of carcinogenic soot—
Someone was always listening to birds,
Thinking of evening or a woman's name,
And trying to get something into words
Which is England, golden now and without blame.

The disappearance of the lines of force
Extending from the Georgian citadels
That uselessly maintain their somber concourse
On the depleted paving stones of Whitehall
Has not stripped out the Admiralty's air
Of sedimented omnicompetence,
All that remains of those four hundred years
It spent outstrategizing Spain and France.
Whether the office space that used to rule
The pink-dyed quarter of the schoolboy's globe
Is subdivided into cubicles
Or storage for old charts and astrolabes
Is less mysterious than how it feels
To spend each workday morning walking down
Gray streets that speak of certainty and will
Now lost. But we will understand it soon.

The windows painted shut and gradually
Opaqued by the accumulated smears
We never managed to get wiped away
Or pried loose in the five neglectful years
We stood or sat in front of them to watch
The fat strays screeching in the garbage cans
Below the terraces where pigeons perched
And squirted their white signatures to stain
The oblong alleyway and squares of grass
That constituted our New York, cut off
From horrors we were sure would come to pass
But knew we wouldn't see the victims of.
The wall-wide panels that we look through now
Let in so much, you'd think that they were meant
For tenants of a city that somehow
Had grown immortal, or indifferent.

ACKNOWLEDGMENTS

I am grateful to the editors of the following magazines, where some of these poems first appeared: *The Atlantic Monthly, Cimarron Review, The Cortland Review, The Hudson Review, The New Republic, The New Criterion, Poetry,* and *Virginia Quarterly Review.*

I am deeply indebted to Princeton University's Council for the Humanities, whose award of a Hodder Fellowship helped me complete this book.

Adam Kirsch is a book critic for the *New York Sun*. His poems and essays have appeared in *The New Yorker*, *The New Republic*, and many other publications. His books include *The Thousand Wells*, which won The New Criterion Poetry Prize; *The Wounded Surgeon*, a study of confessional poetry; and *The Modern Element*, a collection of essays on contemporary poetry.